FOUR KEYS TO SUCCESS

Haneef Salaam

Four Keys to Success

By Haneef Salaam

Cover Created by Bobbi DeNiro

Logo Designs by Andre M. Saunders/Jess Zimmerman

Editor: Anelda L. Attaway

Co-Editor: Haneef Salaam

© 2022 Haneef Salaam

ISBN 978-1-954425-44-6

All rights reserved. This book is protected by the copyright laws of the United States of America. This book may not be copied or reprinted for commercial gain or profit. However, short quotations or occasional page copying for personal or group study is permitted and encouraged. Permission will be granted upon request for Worldwide Distribution. Printed in the United States of America. Published by Jazzy Kitty Publications utilizing Microsoft Publishing Software.

DEDICATION

This book is dedicated to all the people who said I would never be successful and those who told me my life would end by the age of 23 with me dead or in jail. I'm 42 and I AM SUCCESSFUL!!!

Shout out to all my folks from South Bridge; 1 LOVE!

ACKNOWLEDGMENTS

Along my journey to success, there are some people that ensured that I had the morals, principles, knowledge, and opportunities to be successful.

I am forever grateful for my mother and father, which made education for myself and my brother a priority. My parents also ensured we were good people; my father always told me, "Always do things the right way, don't take shortcuts in life." While my mother emphasized, "Always do your best, even if you get older and become a trash man, be the best trash man you can be!" Their words and lessons have stuck with me even today; I use what my parents taught me to help raise my two beautiful daughters, Jakirah and Jakyrah.

My daughters are my motivation to strive for greatness and the reason that I earn an honest living to provide for my family. I have been blessed to have a beautiful wife that has been by my side for over 2 decades. Qaadirah has always been a positive influence and encouraged me to not settle for the streets and be achieve the full potential that so many others have always seen in me. I truly believe that it is important to be positive and give out positive energy as much as possible. Life is better when you live every day in a kind, caring and loving manner. I've come to this philosophy by observing and learning from Qaadirah.

Public Allies Delaware (PADE) played a large part in helping me improve my communication skills, increasing my networking opportunities, and teaching me how to be a nonprofit leader. During my first term with PADE, I met Marla Blunt-Carter, Assistant Professor of Professional Practice at Rutgers University. At the time, she was the Program Director for then Sen. Biden (our current president). Marla taught me about nonprofit operations as well as grant writing. She also encouraged me and always reinforced that I needed to be at the table with the decision-makers. She used to say, "Haneef, when it comes to reentry, you are the expert because you lived it, and that's something that the decision-makers never experienced."

There are so many other people that have had a major impact on my life that I could probably write an entire book on them. I just want everyone, all of my family, friends, colleagues that I have learned from each and every one of you. I love and appreciate you and without all of you, I wouldn't have achieved the levels of success that I have today. So, it is my hope that everyone who reads this book will begin to achieve higher levels of success in their lives!

Peace & Love.

TABLE OF CONTENTS

Introduction……………………………………………….i
First Key – Purpose ..………………………………....01
Second Key – Plan …..………………………………07
Third Key – Focus ..……………………………………14
Fourth Key – Motivational Factor………………...……16
ABOUT THE AUTHOR…………………………..…..18

INTRODUCTION

This book was written to help the reader achieve a higher level of success. I have found that there are four very important principles that everyone must apply if they want to be successful. Purpose, plan, focus, and motivational factors. Anyone that takes the time to identify and clearly understand these principles in their life will be successful.

I want all readers to understand that you must still work hard to succeed. Reading this book alone will not get you there. You must apply the information you learn and implement a good work ethic in your everyday life. Denzel Washington said, "The bridge between goals and accomplishment is hard work and consistency." I strongly believe that if you apply the four keys to success with hard work and consistency, then you will be successful!

FIRST KEY

PURPOSE

"Activity without purpose is the drain of your life" ~ *Tony Robbins*

Everyone has a **PURPOSE** on this Earth. We were not born just to die; we are supposed to do something with our life. Living life without **PURPOSE** clouds your thinking and judgment while creating a void in your life that will cause sadness or confusion. That's why the **FIRST KEY TO SUCCESS is PURPOSE**. You have to know what you want out of your life. You only get one life to live, so you need to know your **PURPOSE** in order to fulfill your **PURPOSE** in life.

Deep down inside, what is it that is going to bring you prosperity, peace and joy? Spend time with yourself and think about it, meditate/pray about it; there is no need to discuss it with anyone because you are the only one that can define your **PURPOSE** in life. Once you are sure of what your **PURPOSE** is write it down on paper. It is critically important to write your **PURPOSE** once you know what it is. This makes your **PURPOSE** a goal; it is just a dream if you don't write your PURPOSE. I believe that your dreams can become your reality. In order to live your dreams, you have to follow the process. In a motivational speech to young actors, Denzel Washington said, "Dreams without goals are just dreams, which ultimately fuel disappointment."

A wise man once told me don't be afraid to dream and have a great vision for your life. Once you see the vision, believe that it will come to pass. If you believe that it will come to pass, then it is on you to expand outside of your comfort zone to possess it. Your ability to define your purpose in life is going to be connected to what you want and expect out of life. If you only see yourself barely getting by all the days of your life, you will subconsciously put yourself in a box. It will be easy for you to settle for less and live a life void of PURPOSE. Your past and your current situation do not change who you truly are and what you're able to accomplish. If you take a victim or blaming perspective, you instantly begin to limit your **PURPOSE**. You will find yourself spending too much of your energy on what other people are doing and why your situation is so bad. You have to learn how to control your thoughts and find a way to be positive about life and positive about your situation. You have to have the confidence in yourself that you can accomplish any goal that you set. Find ways to learn new things and experience new things. It would benefit you to start networking with people you normally wouldn't converse or spend time with. Spend more time around people who have achieved the level of success that you would like for your life. You need to have the faith that you will fulfill your PURPOSE and live the good life the way you see it no matter what happens. I know it to be true that you can achieve anything that you believe you can. Having faith in yourself will allow you to see your vision and purpose in life.

If you don't know your **PURPOSE** or you are unsure complete the following activity. If you do know your purpose, write it in the space provided under ***PURPOSE STATEMENT***

Haneef Salaam

List 5 things that you like doing

LIKES:

1. _____

2. _____

3. _____

4. _____

5. _____

List 5 things that you have learned how to do well with experience

TALENTS:

1. _____

2. _____

3. _____

4. _____

5. _____

List 5 things that you are naturally good at or you can do better than others with less effort

GIFTS:

1. _____

2. _____

3. _____

4. _____

5. _____

As a child, what did you dream of being?

What would you do in life if money was not an issue?

If you had a perfect life, what would you be doing?

VISION:

_____

_____

_____

_____

_____

Think about what you have written and how you feel about your **PURPOSE**.

Write 1 – 2 sentences that describe what you want to do with your life.

PURPOSE STATEMENT:

SECOND KEY

PLAN

"If you fail to plan, then you plan to fail" ~ Harvey McCay

You have to have goals and action steps in line to ensure that you will fulfill your purpose. This starts by creating long-term goals to fulfill your purpose; also creating short-term goals to ensure that you are on track to meet your long-term goals. The example below shows how your goals line up with your Purpose Statement. You will benefit greatly from writing out your long-term and short-term goals.

Example:

✔ Purpose Statement: 1 – 2 sentences that describe what you want to do with your life.

✔ Long-term goal: A long-term goal is something you want to accomplish in the future. Long-term goals require time and planning. They are not something you can do this week or even this year. Long-term goals are usually at least several years away.

✔ Short-term goal: A short-term goal is something you want to do in the near future. The near future can mean today, this week, this month, or even this year. A short-term goal is something you want to accomplish soon.

Your PLAN should be specific and come from the heart. The PLAN to fulfill your purpose should be the steps that you are going to take to be successful. Success isn't how much money you have, the car you drive or how big your house is. Success is the completion or fulfillment of your purpose. So once you've created your purpose statement, you need to create 3 long-term goals that will guide you to fulfilling your purpose. When creating these goals, you have to make sure your goals are SMART (Specific, Measurable, Attainable, Relevant, Time-bound). Making sure that you create SMART goals is the glue to your plan. In addition to your goals, you should also have action steps; 3 specific things that you will do to achieve the goal. Now use the example below to create 3 long-term goals that will help you achieve your purpose.

Example:
LONG-TERM S.M.A.R.T. GOALS

1. Goal: _____
a. Step 1: _____
b. Step 2: _____
c. Step 3: _____

2. Goal: _____
a. Step 1: _____
b. Step 2: _____
c. Step 3: _____

3. Goal: _____
a. Step 1: _____
b. Step 2: _____
c. Step 3: _____

This should help you understand what you need to do in the short term to stay on track and ensure your plan is solid. Now you will repeat the process and create 3 short-term SMART goals, with 3 action steps that you must do to accomplish each goal.

Example

SHORT-TERM S.M.A.R.T. GOALS

4. Goal: _____

a. Step 1: _____

b. Step 2: _____

c. Step 3: _____

5. Goal: _____

a. Step 1: _____

b. Step 2: _____

c. Step 3: _____

6. Goal: _____

a. Step 1: _____

b. Step 2: _____

c. Step 3: _____

Four Keys to Success

Your short-term action steps will help you understand what you should be doing regularly to succeed. Remember your long-term and short-term goals should be focused on your purpose. Once you know your purpose, I've learned that your plan will fall in line. You will get the right job, you will have enough money for material things and money will come and go, but once you are in tune with your purpose in life, you will be prosperous. Life will be easier for you. Les Brown says, "If you do what is hard now, life will get easy. If you do what is easy now, life will get hard."

So now that you have your long and short-term goals, you can lay out your plan on paper. If you don't write your plan out, then it's just a good idea. Write out your plan using the outline provided and check off goals as you accomplish them.

REVIEW YOUR PLAN WHEN YOU WAKE UP EVERY DAY AND BEFORE YOU GO TO SLEEP.

MY SUCCESS PLAN

Dreams without goals are just dreams that ultimately lead to disappointment."

~ Denzel Washington

Purpose Statement: _____

Short-term S.M.A.R.T. goal: _____

Action Steps 1. _____

    2. _____

    3. _____

Short-term S.M.A.R.T. goal: _____

Action Steps 1. _____

    2. _____

    3. _____

Short-term S.M.A.R.T. goal: _____

Action Steps 1. _____

    2. _____

    3. _____

Long-term S.M.A.R.T. goal: _____

Action Steps 1. _____

    2. _____

    3. _____

Four Keys to Success

Long-term S.M.A.R.T. goal: _____

Action Steps 1. _____

2. _____

3. _____

Long-term S.M.A.R.T. goal : _____

Action Steps 1. _____

2. _____

3. _____

THIRD KEY

FOCUS

"You don't get results by focusing on results. You get results by focusing on the actions that produce results"
~Author Unknown

Life is tough and striving for success is not easy. I know personally; I have a criminal background and I was raised in a household where my parents suffered from addiction for most of my life. So I know what it is like to face challenges, get distracted and deal with obstacles that arise in life. Despite all of these things, we have to FOCUS on our *SUCCESS PLAN* to ensure that we are doing what is necessary to be successful. Your success and fulfilling your purpose has to become the most important thing in your life. You must stay mindful of your short-term action steps and ensure you do something every day to get one step closer to your goals. Stay FOCUS on your purpose in life. Eric Thomas says, "Winners FOCUS on winning and losers FOCUS on winners." You have to FOCUS on yourself by investing in yourself. You have to stay FOCUS on yourself and your plan, or you won't be successful and never fulfill your purpose. FOCUS on your *SUCCESS PLAN* is an important key to success. You have to FOCUS on your plan to ensure that your purpose will be fulfilled. If you don't know how to invest in yourself, here are some ideas.

WAYS TO INVEST IN YOURSELF

1. Meditation/Prayer
2. Being around nature
3. Listen to motivational speeches
4. Read (informational, educational, entertainment)
5. Spend quiet time alone
6. Review your *SUCCESS PLAN*
7. Spend time with family
8. Identify a mentor and speak with them regularly
9. Exercise
10. Find hobbies in line with your purpose
11. Continue Education (degree, certification, workshop, seminar)
12. Attend a Conference or Retreat

FOURTH KEY

MOTIVATIONAL FACTOR

"Your motivation must be absolutely compelling in order to overcome the obstacles that will invariably come your way." ~Les Brown

Since we have distractions and obstacles, staying focused is easier said than done; I believe everyone needs a MOTIVATIONAL FACTOR. In order to stay focused on the things we need to do, you must have a MOTIVATIONAL FACTOR. We cannot take shortcuts or avoid obstacles. We must stay focused and stick to that plan. When you feel like you're about to go off track, you need a power greater than yourself that can bring you back and for me, I use my kids. Since my oldest daughter was born on March 24, 2003, I have committed to providing the best life possible for my children. We have already learned that fulfilling your purpose leads to success. So I focus on my plan because of my kids. When it's hard to focus, I think of them when I get distracted, or I face challenges, I think of them. When I think of my daughters and the life I want to provide for them, I get motivated to do anything. My daughters are my MOTIVATIONAL

FACTOR. People will have different MOTIVATIONAL FACTORS; it may not be your children for everyone. For some, it may be spiritual (you want to be pleasing to God). For some, it may be a family member (you want mom or grandma to see you doing good before you go). For others, it may have been a prophesy spoken over you. No matter the person, everyone has a reason to be successful that is bigger than you. Some call this "Your Why"; Why do you want success, why is your purpose what you say it is, why do you do what you do day to day? What is your why? What is your MOTIVATIONAL FACTOR? Once you clearly identify your

MOTIVATIONAL FACTOR, you will have the *4 KEYS TO SUCCESS* and nothing will stop you from fulfilling your purpose. You will be successful in life! Always remember your dreams can be your reality.

"EVERY DAY IS A GREAT DAY TO BE ALIVE"
HANEEF SALAAM

ABOUT THE AUTHOR

Haneef Salaam

Mr. Haneef Salaam is a native Delawarean born and raised in Wilmington. He is engaged in empowering the community and passionate about helping individuals released from prison become positive and productive community members after making that change himself.

Mr. Salaam is currently employed with the ACLU of Delaware as the Smart Justice Campaign Manager. He has also focused on prisoner reentry initiatives for the past 10 years, holding positions such as President of the Delaware Reentry Consortium and Community Facilitator for I-ADAPT, the Governor's reentry initiative. He also started Building Success, LLC, a small business that provides consultation and program planning for nonprofits.

Mr. Salaam is happily married to his wife Qaadirah and has two beautiful daughters, Jakirah and Jakyrah. Mr. Salaam is passionate about helping disadvantaged populations find solutions and ways to overcome their barriers to success. In his free time, Mr. Salaam is a community advocate in Wilmington.

www.ingramcontent.com/pod-product-compliance
Lightning Source LLC
Chambersburg PA
CBHW072040080526
44578CB00007B/544